Charles Simeon of Cambridge

Silhouettes and Skeletons

In collaboration with

CHARLES SIMEON
IN HIS ROOMS AT KING'S COLLEGE

Charles
Simeon of
Cambridge
Silhouettes
and Skeletons

Edited by J E M Cameron

WIPF & STOCK · Eugene, Oregon

CHARLES SIMEON OF CAMBRIDGE
Silhouettes and Skeletons

Wipf & Stock
An Imprint of Wipf and Stock Publishers
199 W. 8th Ave., Suite 3
Eugene, OR 97401

www.wipfandstock.com

PAPERBACK ISBN: 978-1-5326-6353-6
HARDCOVER ISBN: 978-1-5326-6354-3
EBOOK ISBN: 978-1-5326-6355-0

Manufactured in the U.S.A.

First published in the UK 2013.
© Text: John Benton, Julia Cameron, Michael Rees
© Images of silhouettes: Julia E M Cameron
© Portrait of Charles Simeon: By kind permission of the Henry Martyn Centre and
  Ridley Hall, Cambridge.
© Portrait of Henry Martyn: By kind permission of the Master and Fellows
  of St John's College, Cambridge
© Photograph of Simeon's teapot: Bethany Cragg, Holy Trinity Church, Cambridge
© Photograph of Trinity Hall milestone: Arthur Brookes, Trumpington Local History Group
© Sketch of gownsmen assembling for Simeon's funeral: Cambridge University Library
  Manuscripts
© Sketch of Holy Trinity Church in 1803. By kind permission of the Henry Martyn
  Centre, Cambridge.

Designed by Chris Gander

'Charles Simeon was the most influential evangelical in the Church of England during the age of Wilberforce - a powerful influence over successive generations of Cambridge ordinands. Here is an attractive vignette of a great preacher and a great man.'
David Bebbington *Professor of History, University of Stirling*[1]

'As an undergraduate at King's, I was thankful for the teaching of the Gospel of Jesus Christ in the College and the University. The work carried on so faithfully by Charles Simeon, a fellow of King's and vicar of Holy Trinity, continues.'
Jeremy Lefroy *Member of Parliament for Stafford constituency* [2]

'Charles Simeon's commitment to expository preaching, personal godliness, and global mission is inspiring. I pray it will continue to influence evangelical ministry for generations to come.'
Vaughan Roberts *Rector, St Ebbe's Church, Oxford;*
President, Proclamation Trust [3]

'One of the greatest and most persuasive preachers the Church of England has ever known.'
John Stott *(1921-2011) Preacher and author with a global ministry. Chief Architect of The Lausanne Covenant and founder of Langham Partnership.*[4]

'Simeon was a staunch churchman, loving the Church and its services with a devotion which did much to strengthen the bonds between those influenced by the religious revival and those who looked upon it with some misgivings.'
The Rt Revd John Moorman *(1905-1988), Bishop of Ripon and leading ecumenist in A History of the Church of England, 1953.*

'If you knew what his authority and influence were, and how they extended from Cambridge to the most remote corners of England, you would allow that his real sway in the Church was far greater than that of any Primate.'
Lord Macaulay *(1800-1859), Undergraduate at Trinity College, Cambridge in Simeon's time, writing to his sister in 1844.*

CONTENTS

PRINCE OF EVANGELICALS

While Simeon held senior academic roles in the university, he was never given preferment in the Church, and remained throughout 54 years at Holy Trinity as a curate-in-charge. His church wardens created much difficulty for him in his early years, locking the pews, and even locking him out of the church itself. They were angered by the forthright evangelical stance of this young preacher, and sent a formal complaint to the Bishop of Ely.

His death, however, left no uncertainty of the esteem, indeed the widespread affection, in which he came to be held. His funeral was attended by the University Vice-Provost, senior academics, and hundreds of students and graduates. College chapel bells tolled, and shops were closed, as town and gown were united in honour of this 'prince of evangelicals'. It is said that his funeral procession was 'greater than that of the Duke of Wellington'. [5, 6]

his funeral was greater than that of Wellington

Charles Simeon's favourite verse, which appears on his memorial plaque came from the Apostle Paul: I determined to know nothing among you save Jesus Christ and him crucified. (I Corinthians 2:2)

THE CHURCH OF ENGLAND

'When Simeon started preaching in 1782, there was only a handful of evangelical ministers in the Church of England, probably a few dozen. When he finished, 54 years later, one third of C of E pulpits were said to be occupied by evangelicals, and the vast majority of those were men who had been influenced directly by Simeon in Cambridge. His influence on the evangelical cause in the Church of England was absolutely staggering'.

Oliver Barclay: 1986 Annual Lecture of The Evangelical Library (see Further Reading).

TIMELINE OF MAJOR DATES

1759 Born 24 September in Reading, Berkshire, the son of a lawyer

1767–1778 Pupil at Eton College

1779 Entered King's College, Cambridge (January)
Converted to Christ, Easter Day

1782 Appointed as a Fellow of King's College; brief curacy at
St Edward, King & Martyr; appointed to Holy Trinity Church

1784 First meeting with John Wesley

1786 Preached first of many University Sermons in
Great St Mary's Church

1789 Appointed Dean of Divinity

1790 Made Vice-Provost of Cambridge University[7]
Founding by Henry Venn of what would later be referred to
as the Clapham Sect, including Simeon, William Wilberforce,
Thomas Buxton

1792 Began sermon classes

1796 Published Claude's essay and first 100 'skeletons'

1799 Became a founder-member of Africa and the East Mission
(now Church Mission Society) of which he was made an Honorary Governor for Life

1803 Appointed Henry Martyn as curate
(sailed for India 1805; died 1812)

1804 Simeon formed Cambridge branch of the British and Foreign
Bible Society (now The Bible Society), gaining a thundering
attack from the pulpit in St Paul's Cathedral

1809 Founded with others the London Society for Promoting Christianity Amongst the Jews (now the Church's Ministry among
Jewish People, CMJ)

1812 Began conversation parties in his rooms

1817 Began to purchase advowsons, *ie* the right to appoint clergy to churches[8]

1819 First seventeen volumes of *Horae Homileticae* published[9]

1827 Jesus Lane Sunday School begun

1828 Edouart silhouettes created

1833 Full 21 volumes of *Horae Homileticae* published
'Simeon's Trustees' formally created; now with a stake in a total of 180 livings (including the 40 parishes of the Hyndman Trustees, see 1990)

1836 Died 13 November in Cambridge
Buried 19 November in King's College Chapel

1877 Founding of Wycliffe Hall, Oxford, to train Anglican clergy

1881 Founding of Ridley Hall, Cambridge[10]

1881 Henry Martyn Trust established

1885 'Cambridge Seven' sailed for China[11]

1885 Site purchased for Henry Martyn Hall

1887 Henry Martyn Hall opened

1898 Henry Martyn Library opened

1990 Trustees of the Hyndman Trust (originally 'Miss Hyndman's Bounty Trust', in memory of Elizabeth Hyndman, who died in 1835) begin to work closely with Simeon's Trustees[12]

1998 Henry Martyn Library renamed Henry Martyn Centre

2009 Christian Union at Eton College becomes known as the Simeon Society

2012 First symposium, at Wycliffe Hall, Oxford, on the Preaching Methods of Charles Simeon and John Stott[13]

INTRODUCTION

There are in print several fine biographies of Charles Simeon, which we commend. Our aim here is first to give readers a taste of what could be gained from reading a full biography, or reading Simeon's letters,[14] or indeed from digging into his *magnum opus*, the *Horae Homileticae*; and secondly to bring into focus the clear traces of his influence which may still be seen now, two centuries later.

Charles Simeon worked to raise the standard of preaching in local churches. The accompanying silhouettes, painted by Augustin Edouart in 1828, capture beautifully the sheer passion of his preaching. He yearned for the truth of Christ to sink deep into hearts, and pleaded with the Holy Spirit to enlighten minds. His aim as a preacher was to grasp the meaning of scripture in its context, and to apply it effectively in the lives of his hearers.

Simeon found faith in Christ in his first term as an undergraduate at King's College, Cambridge. In 1782, aged 23, he became vicar of the town's Holy Trinity Church, where he remained until his death in 1836.

In 1792 Simeon read the *Essay on the Composition of a Sermon* by Jean Claude (1619-1687) of the French Reformed Church. Through print he discovered a kindred spirit who had lived a century earlier, and this inspired him, also, to write. His sense of history, in a town which had nurtured Reformers, was projected forward in a desire to leave a legacy for younger preachers who would follow him.

Simeon set a model through his writings – both in his published works and his thousands of personal letters. His tone was characteristically fearless, and mostly suffused with grace. This, too, typified the way he engaged with personal opposition.

He took an informed interest in social justice locally and nationally, lending support to his good friend and exact contemporary, William Wilberforce. The legacy of his work with the Clapham Sect (see Timeline) is a study on its own. His ministry, in this sense, would now be described as holistic.[15] In addition, he practised and encouraged a deep concern for world mission, particularly among Jewish people, and in India, where his curate Henry Martyn served. The legacy of Henry Martyn, his son in Christ, barely touched on here, is of massive significance. Martyn was one of several Cambridge men who sailed for India with whom Simeon kept in touch.[16]

Simeon had grasped Scripture's over-arching story – that of a missionary Father's plan to send his missionary Son to bring redemption from sin, and to empower the Church for our mission through his missionary Holy Spirit, until he should return. Simeon was gripped by this, and his preaching breathed it.

Simeon lent energetic support to the founding of the British and Foreign Bible Society in 1804, despite severe opposition in academic and ecclesiastical circles, based in part on the absence of any liturgy bound with scripture, to help a reader interpret the text. Hugh Evan Hopkins cites the now bemusing objection that: 'The Bible should not be industriously put into [a working man's] hands, as it is too obscure for his rude understanding.' In 1808 the Pennsylvania Bible Society was founded, followed in 1816 by the American Bible Society (ABS), then the Bible Societies of Australia and New South Wales. Today the work of the United Bible Societies (UBS, founded 1946) reaches into 200 nations and territories.

We trust this collection of brief writings will help a new generation to glimpse what we owe, under God, to the obedience and dogged work of Charles Simeon. His 'skeletons' exemplify the care he took to nurture new preachers in their craft; his meeting with John Wesley shows his desire for unity in the gospel, wherever that is possible, without compromising on the great primary truths. The anniversary prayers with which he is still remembered signify the weight of his contribution to the Anglican Communion.

His writing and the records of his preaching left a deep impression on John Stott, as they have, for example, on John Piper, Dick Lucas and Vaughan Roberts. Here we will see how, in God's purposes, the ripples of Simeon's influence continue to reach down the years, and across the world.

As we sketch out this story, we see how the Cambridge Inter-Collegiate Christian Union (CICCU) has played a central role in its unfolding. Where those featured have links to Cambridge University, or specifically to the CICCU, this is noted briefly. Future church history will add further chapters. ♦

SIMEON'S SKELETONS

To assist young preachers, Charles Simeon published *Helps to Composition; or six hundred skeletons of sermons; several being the substance of sermons preached before the university*. The work became popularly known as *Simeon's Skeletons*.[17]

Simeon defines the skeleton of a discourse in the following way: 'It should be not merely a sketch or outline, but a full draft, containing all the component parts of a Sermon, and all the ideas necessary for the illustration of them, at the same time that it leaves scope for the exercise of industry and genius in him who uses it.'

The first volume of his *Skeletons* includes the essay on the composition of sermons which Simeon greatly admired by Jean Claude, who ministered 'upwards of forty years with great acceptance, first at St Afrique, afterwards at Nimes, and lastly at Charenton.' But in his preface to the work, while recommending Claude's essay, Simeon imparts something of his own approach to preaching.

Simeon explained that all his skeletons were 'intended to illustrate one general rule; namely how texts may be treated in a *natural* manner.' He goes on, 'The Author has invariably proposed to himself three things as indispensably necessary in every discourse: UNITY in the design, PERSPICUITY in the arrangement, and SIMPLICITY in the diction.' In referring to diction, he means the language and delivery of the sermon. In a footnote he says, 'It is not intended by 'simplicity of diction' that the language should never be figurative or sublime: the language ought certainly to rise to the subject, and should be on many occasions nervous and energetic: but still, it is a vicious taste to be aiming at, what is called, fine language: the language should not elevate the subject, but the subject, it.'

it is a vicious taste to aim at fine language

In telling the reader how the skeletons for his sermons were composed, Simeon explains that he focuses on four things.

1 The meaning of the text

'As soon as the subject is chosen, the first enquiry is, 'What is the principal scope and meaning of the text?' In considering this matter, he takes as his example Jeremiah 31.18-20.

> 'I have surely heard Ephraim's moaning: "You disciplined me like an unruly calf, and I have been disciplined. Restore me, and I will return, because you are the LORD my God. After I strayed, I repented; after I came to understand, I beat my breast. I was ashamed and humiliated because I bore the disgrace of my youth." Is not Ephraim my dear son, the child in whom I delight? Though I often speak against him, I still remember him. Therefore my heart yearns for him; I have great compassion for him,' declares the LORD.

nothing is to be introduced which does not reflect light upon the main subject

To open his thesis, he writes:

'Upon examination, it appears to be a soliloquy of the Deity, expressing what he had seen in the workings of Ephraim's mind, and declaring the emotions which the fight of his penitent child had occasioned within his own [heart].'

> This is the subject of Skeleton 9 in the collection which Simeon entitles *The reflections of a penitent*. He goes on, 'Having ascertained this, nothing is to be introduced into any part of the discourse, which does not in some way or other, reflect light upon the main subject.'

2 The parts of the text

The next enquiry is: 'Of what parts does the text consist, or into what parts may it be most easily and naturally resolved?' With respect to the sample text from Jeremiah, Simeon says,

> 'Here an obvious division occurs: it is evident that the text contains, *first*, the reflections of a true penitent; and *secondly*,

the reflections of God over him. This division being made, the discussion of the two parts must be undertaken in order.'

The text is then to be investigated with these subjects in mind and Simeon encourages us to let the text speak for itself.

'If the text did not contain any important matter, it would then be proper, and even necessary, to enter in [a] general manner into the subject: but if the text itself afford ample means of elucidating the point that is under discussion, it is always best to adhere to that.'

3 The application of the text

In describing how to apply the text, we see Simeon as evangelist and pastor:

'The nature of the application must depend in some measure on the subject discussed, and on the state of the congregation to whom it is addressed. Where there are many who make a profession of godliness, it will be necessary to pay some attention to them, and to accommodate the subject in part to their state, in a way of conviction, consolation, encouragement etc. But where the congregation is almost entirely composed of persons who are walking in the broad way of worldliness and indifference, it may be proper to suit the application to them alone.'

4 The introduction to the text

This is spoken of as 'the exordium', and, while it comprises the first part of the sermon, it should, according to Simeon, be the last part to be composed. Here Simeon refers to Claude's directions: 'The principal design of an exordium is to attract or excite the affections of the audience – to stir up their attention – and to prepare them for the particular matters we are about to treat.'

Both Simeon and Claude see the introduction as critical for effective preaching. Claude writes with some fervour:

'We cannot approve, then, of the custom of English preachers, who enter immediately into the literal explication of the text, and make it serve as an exordium... Least of all do we approve of the custom of some of our own preachers, who, intending to explain the text, or to make some reflections throughout the whole sermon, enter immediately into the matter without any exordiums at all. I am persuaded they are induced to do thus only for the sake of avoiding the difficulty of composing an exordium, that is, in one word, only for the sake of indulging their idleness and negligence.'

After explaining his method of composing a skeleton for a sermon, Simeon considers whether or not to describe to listeners the divisions of a passage of scripture. He argues that while this is not essential, 'it is not to be thought ... a matter of indifference: the minds of the generality are not capable of tracing the connexion and coherence of a discourse: their attention will flag; they will lose much of what they hear; and have no clue whereby to recover it: whereas the mention of an easy and natural division will relieve their minds, assist their memories, and enable them to "mark, learn, and inwardly digest" the word.'

an easy and natural division will assist their memories

The use of skeletons

Simeon then moves on to recommend the use of skeletons for preaching.

'It is not possible to say what is the best mode of preaching for every individual, because the talents of men are so various, and the extent of their knowledge so different. It seems at all events expedient that a young minister should for some years pen his sermons, in order that he may attain a proper mode of expressing his thoughts, and accustom himself to the obtaining of clear, comprehensive, and judicious views of his subject: but that he should always continue to write every word of his discourses seems by no means necessary. Not that it is at any time expedient for him to deliver an unpremeditated harangue: this would be unsuitable to the holy and important office which he stands up to discharge.

'But there is a medium between such extemporaneous effusions and a servile adherence to what is written: there is a method recommended by the highest authorities, which, after we have written many hundred sermons, it may not be improper to adopt: the method referred to is, to draw out a full plan or skeleton of the discourse, with the texts of Scripture which are proper to illustrate or enforce the several parts, and then to express the thoughts in such language as may occur at the time. This plan, if it have some disadvantage in point of accuracy or elegance, has, on the other hand, great advantages over the written sermon: it gives a minister an opportunity of speaking with far more effect to the hearts of men, and of addressing himself to their passions, as well by his looks and gesture, as by his words.'

draw out a full plan or skeleton of the discourse

The test of a sermon, indeed the touchstone for every endeavour, was this: 'Does it uniformly tend TO HUMBLE THE SINNER? TO EXALT THE SAVIOUR? TO PROMOTE HOLINESS?'

He concludes, 'Let smaller differences of sentiment be overlooked, and all unite in vindicating the great doctrines of SALVATION BY GRACE THROUGH FAITH IN CHRIST.'

Based on the second edition of Simeon's Skeletons *published by Luke Hansard & Sons, London, 1808. Scripture quotation updated to New International Version (1984).*

♦ ♦ ♦

SIMEON'S MINISTRY

Charles Simeon, a man of deep and disciplined Christian devotion, was a shrewd judge of character, particularly of those who might serve in the Church's ministry. He had creative flair; he was an entrepreneur for the gospel; he set high standards for himself. These, together with his sheer creativity, have left a lasting legacy.

Charles Simeon founded a Trust for nominating 'gospel men', as he would term them, to be vicars of local parishes. In those days advowsons, or patronages, could be bought and sold, and Simeon, William Wilberforce, and other friends took advantage of this, as a means of purchasing spheres of influence for the gospel. Writing to a clergyman in 1817, Simeon could ask, 'What is your object? Is it to win souls?' Simeon and his friends originally purchased 26 such livings. Simeon's Trustees now have an involvement with some 180 parishes.[18]

Simeon relied on the Bible alone for all his spiritual understanding, and to prepare for his preaching and teaching. His Bible study, prayer and preparation took up around four hours each day. He loved the 'doctrines of grace' – and he would fearlessly ask his fellow clergy if they were preaching Christ and expounding the Scriptures. He hated rigid systems of doctrine as he could not find such in his Bible. 'Be Bible Christians,' he wrote, 'not systems Christians.'

He pioneered the training of ordinands. Simeon became Vicar of Holy Trinity Church, Cambridge, in 1782. He learnt much from older Christians, but received no preparation for how to be a vicar. He was concerned for the clergy he had himself seen through to ordination, and from 1796 held annual houseparties for clergymen, to better equip them. Ahead of his time, he always wanted their wives to come with them – 'the importance of the wives' ministry must never be overlooked.'

Simeon pioneered the training of ordinands

He became an indefatigable preacher and evangelist. During the three-month period from 18 May to 19 August 1798 he reckoned he had preached 75 times, to a total of 87,310 people!

He pioneered evening services, and expanded capacity. Simeon started a 6pm Sunday service in 1790, producing his own hymnbook (340 hymns), and purchasing a barrel-organ in 1793. During the first half of his ministry, 100 at Sunday worship was considered a good attendance. But by 1833 the crowds were pouring in, and Holy Trinity could seat 1100, with balconies on three sides.

He introduced home groups. Knowing how well people learn when they have to respond in a group, or lead a session, Simeon encouraged home groups or 'societies', and would visit these in turn. It is reckoned that at the height of this movement, 120 people participated in such groups. If he sensed a group had lost its direction, he closed it down.

He encouraged family devotions. While having no family himself, he conducted prayers with his college gyp and bedder.[19]

He founded a Visiting Society to bring relief to the poor. He trained its members to share and teach the Christian faith while they took round food and other provisions. He set up a Provident Bank – we would call it a Credit Union. The winter of 1788/89 was a bad one, and many villages suffered from rising bread prices. Simeon with his own money bought bread at the inflated price and distributed to roughly 24 villages near Cambridge at the old price.

He prayed with passion as he preached with passion. Simeon saw the special role of public prayer. When Simeon led God's people in worship and prayer from the vicar's stall in Holy Trinity, he knew himself to be closer to God than at any other time. He believed 'as is the minister, so are the people'. '*Pray* the prayers,' he urged his congregation as they followed the liturgy, 'don't read them only.'

Simeon's wider legacy

Charles Simeon founded with others, in 1799, what is now known as the Church Mission Society, and in 1809 what is now known as the Church's Ministry among Jewish People (CMJ).[20] He also started the first Bible Society branch in Cambridge. He wanted men to press their gifts into service in the most effective ways, in the UK or overseas. Many pioneers of the Christian Church in Commonwealth countries owed their faith to him. The Sunday School in Jesus Lane, run by students in response to Simeon's ministry, is regarded as having a special place in the founding, forty years after Simeon's death, of the CICCU, which would have an influence on the church in almost every country in the world.[21]

In recent times, comparisons have been drawn between Charles Simeon and John Stott (1921-2011); the parallels between these pastor-theologians are striking. Both were products of leading English public schools; both Cambridge men; both bachelors whose life's ministry was based in one church.[22] John Stott served as chief architect of *The Lausanne Covenant* (1974) which is widely regarded as having re-awakened the evangelical social conscience, so eloquently exemplified in the lives of men like Simeon and Wilberforce.[23] His own magisterial contribution through preaching, writing, ministering to students, nurturing young preachers, and living out a commitment to see the gospel penetrate the working world, the geographical world, and the world of ideas, all add weight to his popularly being known as 'the second Simeon'.[24] [25]

John Stott wrote and spoke often of the way Simeon had shaped his thinking from his own student days.[26] So it is not fanciful for us to trace the line of Simeon's influence, under God, on into the four flourishing ministries which John Stott either founded, or helped to foster, namely: (i) Langham Partnership, (ii) the Lausanne Movement, (iii) the International Fellowship of Evangelical Students (IFES) and (iv) the London Institute for Contemporary Christianity (LICC).[27] The same could be said of Dick Lucas with his ministry in the City of London and his founding of the Proclamation Trust.

THE PATTERN DEVELOPS

'The Bishop of Peterborough, and some other Bishops, refused to ordain anyone of evangelical persuasion. Simeon's men were banished to remote country parishes where nobody thought they could do any harm. But in these remote places, young men were converted through their minister, came to Cambridge, usually to Queens' College and sat under Charles Simeon. So the cycle developed. That is how they captured one third of the Church of England pulpits. If you know the recent history of the evangelical movement in the Church of Scotland, you will see an analogy.'

Barclay: 1986 *Op cit* (slightly abbreviated)

HENRY MARTYN

Henry Martyn (1781-1812) a graduate and Fellow of St John's College, was one of several highly gifted students who came under the influence of the gospel at Holy Trinity. Martyn started coming to Holy Trinity regularly after his father died. In 1803 Simeon introduced Martyn to Charles Grant, a Director of the East India Company and recommended him as a Chaplain. Henry Martyn sailed for India in 1805, and would complete his life's work in seven years. His contribution was enormous. [28] [29]

Vaughan Roberts notes:[30]

> Simeon was well aware of the multiplying effect of [student] ministry: if a young man he taught was gripped by the gospel and then ordained, he could be the means of many others coming to Christ and being discipled. As a student entered Holy Trinity, he was heard to comment, "Here come six hundred people."[31] On another occasion, he said, "Many of those who hear me are legions in themselves because they are going forth to preach, or else to fill stations of influence in society. In that view, I look on my position here as the highest and most important in the kingdom, nor would I exchange it for any other."[32]

no one looks at me as he does – he never takes his eyes off me

Two days before Henry Martyn died, Simeon travelled to London to receive a portrait of him that had just arrived from India.[33] He was moved by Martyn's evident decline. He would point to the painting and say to guests; 'There! See that blessed man! What an expression of countenance! No one looks at me as he does – he never takes his eyes off me; and seems always to be saying, "Be serious – be in earnest. Don't trifle – don't trifle." And I won't trifle – I *won't* trifle.'

Simeon loved Henry Martyn like a son, and news of his death was a painful blow. He raised a memorial plaque to him in the Holy Trinity Chancel, recording his service at Holy Trinity and his sailing with the East India Company, followed by the lines:

There having faithfully chosen the work of an Evangelist,
Preaching the Gospel of a Crucified Redeemer,
In translating the Holy Scriptures into the Oriental languages,
And in defending the Christian Faith in the heart of Persia
Against the united talents of the most learned Mohamedans,
He died at Tokat on the 16th October, 1812
In the 31st year of his Age.

The chief monuments which he left of his piety and talents are
Translations of the New Testament
Into the Hindoostanee and Persian languages
And by these, 'he, being dead, yet speaketh'.

♦ ♦ ♦

MEETING WITH JOHN WESLEY

On 20 December 1784, the young Charles Simeon rode over to Hinxworth, in Hertfordshire, to meet John Wesley, by now 81 years of age. It was to prove for Simeon a formative encounter.

Simeon was 'no friend to systematisers in Theology'

There was much discussion in these years on the merits of Arminianism (as espoused by the Wesleys) and Calvinism (as espoused by George Whitefield and the Countess of Huntingdon).[34] Simeon was 'no friend to systematisers in Theology'[35], and preferred personal study of scripture over reading theological writings. He did not warm to divisions among believing Christians.

This is how he recalls the meeting years later, the distance in time perhaps accounting for the comparative brevity we find in the recollected responses of Wesley.

> **Simeon** Sir, I understand that you are called an Arminian; and I have been sometimes called a Calvinist; and therefore I suppose we are to draw daggers. But before I consent to begin the combat, with your permission I will ask you a few questions, not for impertinent curiosity, but for real instruction... Pray, Sir, do you feel yourself a depraved creature, so depraved that you would never have thought of turning to God if God had not first put it into your heart?
>
> **Wesley** Yes, I do indeed.
>
> Simeon And do you utterly despair of recommending yourself to God by anything you can do; and look for salvation solely through the blood and righteousness of Christ?
>
> **Wesley** Yes, solely through Christ.
>
> **Simeon** But, Sir, supposing you were first saved by Christ, are you not somehow or other to save yourself afterwards by your own works?

Wesley No; I must be saved by Christ from first to last.

Simeon Allowing then that you were first turned by the grace of God, are you not in some way or other to keep yourself by your own power?

Wesley No.

Simeon What then, are you to be upheld every hour and every moment by God, as much as an infant in its mother's arms?

Wesley Yes, altogether.

Simeon And is all your hope in the grace and mercy of God to preserve you unto his heavenly kingdom?

Wesley Yes, I have no hope but in him.

Simeon Then, Sir, with your leave, I will put up my dagger again; for this is all my Calvinism; this is my election, my justification by faith, my final perseverance: it is, in substance, all that I hold, and as I hold it; and therefore, if you please, instead of searching out terms and phrases to be a ground of contention between us, we will cordially unite in those things wherein we agree.

Wesley's record in his Journal suggested he, too, had appreciated the encounter:

'Mon. 20 – I went to Hinxworth, where I had the satisfaction of meeting Mr Simeon, Fellow of King's College in Cambridge. He has spent some times with Mr Fletcher, at Madeley: two kindred souls; much resembling each other, both in fervour of spirit and in the earnestness of their address. He gave me the pleasing information, that there are three parish churches in Cambridge wherein true scriptural religion is preached; and several young gentlemen who are happy partakers of it.[36] I preached in the evening on Gal. vi. 14.' [37]

CHARLES SIMEON'S CAMBRIDGE

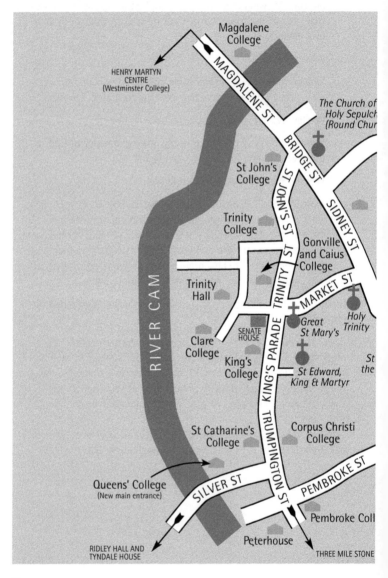

Magdalene College

MAGDALENE ST

HENRY MARTYN CENTRE (Westminster College)

The Church of Holy Sepulch (Round Chur

BRIDGE ST

St John's College

ST JOHN'S ST

SIDNEY ST

Trinity College

Gonville and Caius College

TRINITY ST

Trinity Hall

RIVER CAM

MARKET ST

Holy Trinity

Clare College

SENATE HOUSE

Great St Mary's

King's College

KING'S PARADE

St Edward, King & Martyr

St the

St Catharine's College

Corpus Christi College

Queens' College (New main entrance)

TRUMPINGTON ST

SILVER ST

PEMBROKE ST

Pembroke Coll

RIDLEY HALL AND TYNDALE HOUSE

Peterhouse

THREE MILE STONE

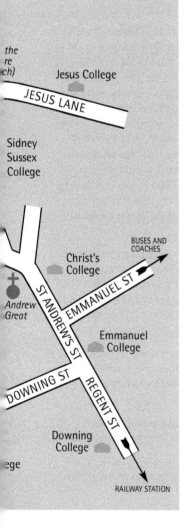

the
re
ch)
Jesus College

JESUS LANE

Sidney
Sussex
College

Christ's
College

BUSES AND
COACHES

Andrew
Great

ST ANDREW'S ST

EMMANUEL ST

Emmanuel
College

DOWNING ST

REGENT ST

Downing
College

ege

RAILWAY STATION

CHRISTIAN HERITAGE

Much is to be learned of the town's spiritual history and legacy from Christian Heritage, based in the Round Church (see map). Open daily. For news of lectures, guided walks throughout the year, and its summer school, go to –
www.christianheritage.org.uk

SUNDAY WORSHIP

Holy Trinity Church welcomes visitors to Sunday services.

Other evangelical churches in the city centre include St Andrew the Great (StAG), Eden Baptist Church and Cambridge Presbyterian Church.

EARLIER HISTORY

St Edward's is known as 'the cradle of the Reformation.' Thomas Bilney, Robert Barnes and Hugh Latimer preached here; the same pulpit is used now.

Holy Trinity had a Puritan tradition, with such Puritan leaders as Richard Sibbes, Thomas Goodwin and John Preston.

 Main entrance

Not to scale

SIMEON'S SILHOUETTES

Simeon was an eccentric preacher, with his own unique mannerisms. He could be easily parodied, and often was. It is not surprising that he should catch the attention of the French silhouettist, Augustin Edouart.

Augustin Amant Constant Fidèle Edouart (1789-1861) was born in Dunkirk, and was decorated under Napoleon. He left France in 1814 to settle first in London. In 1825 he alighted on the silhouette, simple and arresting, as his favoured means of art; he toured England, cutting out images in black card of royalty, nobility, gentry, politicians, and people of note in the professions, the military and the navy. In 1829 he arrived in Edinburgh where he remained for three years, producing some 5,000 images in that period alone. He sailed to New York in 1839, and spent the next ten years in the United States, mainly in New England. He later returned to his native France.

he alighted on the silhouette, simple and arresting

Edouart kept copies of all his work, which reached the rare total of over 100,000 silhouettes. Some of these were lost when he sailed back to Europe in 1849 on the *Oneida*, which was shipwrecked. The New York Historical Society retains a collection of all his remaining American silhouettes. Edouart's book, *A Treatise on Silhouette Likenesses*, containing many illustrations, was published in 1835.[38]

It is not clear who named the Simeon silhouettes, nor indeed whether all eight were at one stage given names. Six names have travelled down to us. To these, 'Applying' and 'Ascribing' have been added by the Editor.

A ninth image, an engraving dating from the 1820s or early 1830s, by an otherwise unrecognised artist, is often grouped with the silhouettes. We include it here as a prelude to the preaching sequence. The title 'Returning' is not original.

 Returning He walks purposefully back to church from his rooms in King's College.

Edouart's silhouettes

 Imploring His hands are together in prayer, as he leads the congregation to the throne of grace.

 Acquiring His finger points to the text, with his left hand holding his glasses while he examines the scriptures carefully, as his authority.

 Expounding Arms extended, he uses fingers on both hands to enumerate points from the passage.

 Imparting His right hand points to scripture; his left, as it were, extends its truth and meaning to the congregation.

 Entreating His right hand extended, upturned, with thumb and forefinger almost meeting, encapsulates the reasoned gospel, in its simplicity.

 Applying His left hand rests on the text, and his right arm points to his listeners.

 Ascribing His left hand points to Scripture, his right heavenward, to its author and inspirer.

 Concluding He stands back in the pulpit, having delivered his charge before God, with reason and with passion.

◆ ◆ ◆

ANNIVERSARY PRAYERS

Each year on 13 November, the anniversary of Charles Simeon's death, the following prayer is used in Choral Evensong at King's College Chapel:

> Almighty and everlasting God, who by thy holy servant, Charles Simeon, didst mould the lives of many that they might go forth and teach others also; mercifully grant that as through evil report and good report he ceased not to preach thy saving Word, so we may never be ashamed of the Gospel of Jesus Christ, our Lord, who with Thee and the Holy Spirit, liveth and reigneth one God world without end. Amen.

The collect for that day in the Church of England Common Worship also remembers him:

> Eternal God, who raised up Charles Simeon to preach the good news of Jesus Christ and inspire your people in service and mission: grant that we with all your Church may worship the Saviour, turn in sorrow from our sins and walk in the way of holiness, through Jesus Christ Your Son, our Lord who is alive and reigns with you in the unity of the Holy Spirit one God, now and for ever. Amen.

He is also still remembered in the Episcopal Church in the USA and the Anglican Church in Canada on 12 November, in the collect for the Lesser Feasts and Fasts. The discrepancy of dates lies in an original error in F L Cross: *Oxford Dictionary of the Christian Church* (1957). It was corrected in the Church of England by the General Synod in the late 1970s, at the prompting of Bishop Timothy Dudley-Smith[39] and Canon Michael Rees. However, churches in North America did not make the change.

◆ ◆ ◆

APPENDIX 1[40]

Simeon's prayer before he preached

The following was written out, perhaps by a congregation member, and lodged, unsigned, with the note:

'This prayer was always said by beloved Mr Simeon before his sermon, and [is] copied from his Bible.'

O God who hast caused all Holy Scriptures to be written for our hearing, be with us now to sanctify unto us the truths that shall be derived from them. Be with us especially to enlighten our minds by thy Holy Spirit; and by the mighty working of thy power bring into the way of truth all such as have erred and are deceived. Be pleased, also, O Lord, to strengthen such as do stand, and comfort and help the weak hearted, and raise them up that fall, and finally to beat down Satan under all our feet.

All this we humbly ask in the name and for the sake of Jesus Christ our Lord. Amen

THE TRUTH AT BOTH EXTREMES

Simeon believed: 'The truth is not in the middle, and not in one extreme; but in both extremes' even if you cannot reconcile them. He was aware how his critics would respond. 'Go to Aristotle,' they would say, 'and learn the golden mean.' 'But my brother,' Simeon would reply, 'I formerly studied Aristotle, and I liked him much. I have since read Paul, and caught something of his strange notions, oscillating [not vacillating] from pole to pole. Sometimes I am a high Calvinist, at other times a low Arminian, so if extremes will please you, I am your man. Only remember, it is not one extreme that we are to go to, but both extremes.'

Carus, p600. Quoted by John Stott in his Introduction to *Evangelical Preaching* (slightly abbreviated). See Further Reading.

APPENDIX 2

Simeon's Senior Wranglers

Charles Simeon drew around him some of the most able minds across the university, as is evidenced here. He laid stress on undergraduates working hard. The following men, all regular worshippers at Holy Trinity or in some sympathy with Simeon's teaching, attained the distinction of 'Senior Wrangler', a term unique to Cambridge to identify the top mathematician of the year.

This list, while not comprehensive in its information, gives a flavour of why Simeon should refer to a student as 'six hundred people'. Simeon evidently enjoyed engagement with sharp minds. 'I have had six Senior Wranglers dine with me at once, all pious men,' he wrote in 1827. The years listed indicate the date on which the title Senior Wrangler was attained.

1774 Isaac Milner (Queens'): Jacksonian Professor (1783-1792); President of Queens' (1788-1820) and Dean of Carlisle (1791-1820).

1778 William Farish (Magdalene): Professor of Chemistry (1794-1813) and Jacksonian Professor (1813-1837).

1783 Francis Wollaston (Sidney Sussex): Fellow of the Royal Society from 1786; Jacksonian Professor (1792-1813); Rector of Cold Norton and Archdeacon of Essex (1813-1823).

1785 William Lax (Trinity): Vicar of Marsworth, Bucks and of St Ippolyts, Herts, where he erected an observatory. Lowdean Professor of Astronomy, Cambridge (1795-1836).

1788 John Brinkley (Caius): Professor of Astronomy at Trinity College Dublin; Astronomer Royal for Ireland; Bishop of Cloyne (1826-1835); President of the Royal Astronomical Society (1831-1833).

1790 Bewick Bridge (Peterhouse): Professor of Mathematics at the East India Company College, Haileybury (1806-1816); Vicar of Cherry Hinton, Cambs (1816-1833); founder of its Primary School (1832).

1798 Thomas Sowerby (Queens'): Curate of Holy Trinity (died 1808).

1801 Henry Martyn (St John's): Curate of Holy Trinity; Chaplain in East India Company (died 1812).

1804 John Kaye (Christ's): Master of Christ's (1814-1816); Regius Professor of Divinity 1816-20; Bishop of Bristol (1820-1827); Bishop of Lincoln (1827-1853).

1807 Henry Gipps (St John's): Vicar of St Peter, Hereford from 1824; Conservative Party Politician and MP for Canterbury 1852-53. Died 1859.

1808 Henry Bickersteth (Caius): Master of the Rolls from 1836; given peerage as 1st Baron Langdale. Initiated the founding of the Public Record Office. Died 1851.

1812 Cornelius Neale (St John's): Ordained 1822 to a curacy in Leicester. Died of consumption 1823.

1819 Joshua King (Trinity): President of Queens' (1832-1857); Lucasian Professor (1839-1849). Regarded by some as a 'second Newton' but regrettably he left no published material.

1828 Charles Perry (Trinity): First Bishop of Melbourne (1847-1876); founder of Wycliffe Hall, Oxford and Ridley Hall, Cambridge, both of which opened after he died.

1835 Henry Cotterill (St John's): Chaplain to the Madras Presidency (from 1837); Bishop of Grahamstown, South Africa (1856-71); Bishop of Edinburgh (1871-86).

Charles Simeon's teapot and the Windsor chair from his rooms in King's College, both central to his conversation parties, are kept in Holy Trinity Church. His umbrella (one of the first in England) is also there. (See Christian Heritage tours.)

APPENDIX 3

Simeon's advice to undergraduates on how to get a good degree

I always say to my young friends: 'Your success in the Senate House depends much on the care you take of the three-mile stone out of Cambridge. If you go every day, and see that no-one has taken it away, and go quite round it to watch lest anyone has damaged its farthest side, you will be best able to read steadily all the time you are at Cambridge. If you neglect, woe betide your degree. Yes! Exercise, constant and regular and ample, is absolutely essential to a reading man's success.'

From Abner Brown's *Conversations* p126 (see Further Reading).

The Trinity Hall milestones were so called as the legacy which paid for them was administered by William Warren, a Fellow of Trinity Hall. He used the southwest buttress of Great St Mary's as his reference point. The stones carry the Crescent arms of Trinity Hall.

This milestone was removed while Hauxton Road was re-aligned, for the construction of Addenbrooke's Road. It was then replaced close to its original location.

APPENDIX 4

Simeon's charge to his Patronage Trust

We who are now Simeon's Trustees believe it will be of value to draw attention to the CHARGE which Charles Simeon gave to his Trustees when he set up his patronage trust in 1833. Whenever a new Trustee or Assessor is appointed, this Charge is read:

IN THE NAME AND IN THE PRESENCE OF ALMIGHTY GOD, I give the following charge to all my Trustees and to all who shall succeed them in the Trust to the remotest ages. I implore them for the Lord Jesus Christ's sake, and I charge them also before that adorable Saviour who will call them into Judgment for their execution of the Trust:

I charge them also before that adorable Saviour

First, that they be very careful, whenever they shall be called upon to fill up a vacancy in this Trust, which they must invariably do within three months of a vacancy occurring, that they elect no one who is not a truly pious and devoted man, a man of God in deed and in truth, who with his piety combines a solid judgement and a perfectly independent mind. I place this first, because a failure in this one particular would utterly defeat, and that in perpetuity too, all that I have sought to do for God and for immortal souls.

Secondly, that, when they shall be called upon to appoint to a living, they consult nothing but the welfare of the people for whom they are to provide, and whose eternal interests have been confided in them. They must on no account be influenced by any solicitation of the great and powerful, or by any partiality towards any one on account of the largeness of his family or the smallness of his income. They must be particularly on their guard against petitions from the parishes to be provided for, whether on behalf of a Curate that has laboured among them, or of any other individual. They must examine carefully, and

they must be particularly on their guard against petitions

judge as before God, how far any person possesses the qualifications suited to the particular Parish, and by that consideration alone must they be determined in their appointment of him.

Signed by me this 18th day of March in the year of our Lord one thousand eight hundred and thirty-three.

Cha.ᵉ Simeon

CHARLES SIMEON

♦ ♦ ♦

APPENDIX 5
WEBSITES

A projection forward by two centuries. This list captures only the churches and ministries appearing in these pages. It does not attempt to survey all the traces of Simeon's influence under God.

CHARLES SIMEON AND HENRY MARTYN Simeon's Trustees (UK, with Hyndman Trust) *www.simeons.org.uk* Henry Martyn Centre *www.martynmission.cam.ac.uk* Taylor University, IN: Simeon pages *www.charlessimeon.com** The Simeon Trust (US) *www.simeon.org*

CHURCH (global and local) Anglican Mainstream *www.anglican-mainstream.net* Reform *www.reform.org.uk* Holy Trinity Church, Cambridge *www.htcambridge.org.uk* All Souls, Langham Place, London *www.allsouls.org* All Saints, Lolworth *www.honeyhill.org/lolworth.htm* St Edward, King and Martyr, Cambridge *http://sainteds.wordpress.com* King's College Chapel *www.kings.cam.ac.uk* Great St Mary's *www.gsm.cam.ac.uk*

STUDENT MOVEMENTS Cambridge Inter-Collegiate Christian Union (CICCU) *www.ciccu.org.uk* Universities and Colleges Christian Fellowship (UCCF) *www.uccf.org.uk* International Fellowship of Evangelical Students (IFES) *www.ifesworld.org*

TRAINING Ridley Hall, Cambridge *www.ridley.cam.ac.uk* Wycliffe Hall, Oxford *www.wycliffe.ox.ac.uk* London Institute for Contemporary Christianity *www.licc.org.uk* Proclamation Trust *www.proctrust.org.uk* '9:38' *www.ninethirtyeight.org*

MISSION (national and international) African Enterprise *www.aeinternational.org* Church's Ministry among Jewish People (CMJ) *www.cmj.org.uk* Church Mission Society (CMS) *www.cms-uk.org* Crosslinks *www.crosslinks.org* Langham Partnership *www.langham.org* Titus Trust *www.titustrust.org* The Lausanne Movement *www.lausanne.org* United Bible Societies *www.unitedbiblesocieties.org*

*Includes 2004 inaugural 'Charles Simeon Lecture' given, unsurprisingly, by John Stott. While evidently frail, Stott pays a perceptive 30-minute tribute to Simeon, his lifelong mentor in ministry, from student days onwards.

Born Sept. 24th, 1759.

Revd. Char

Buried in King's College

les Simeon,

Chapel, Nov. 19th, 1836.   Died Nov. 13th, 1836.

P.T.O.

SIMEON'S MEMORIAL

The memorial plaque in
Holy Trinity Church

In Memory of
THE REV. CHARLES SIMEON M.A.
Senior Fellow of King's College,
and fifty-four years Vicar of this parish;
who, whether as the ground of his own hopes,
or as the subject of all his ministrations,
determined
to know nothing but
JESUS CHRIST AND HIM CRUCIFIED
1 Cor. ii.2

John Stott, as a public mark of the influence of Simeon on his ministry, asked for the same wording of Simeon's aspirations to appear on his own headstone. His grave is found in the churchyard at Dale, Pembrokeshire, near his writing retreat 'The Hookses'.

FURTHER READING

For a growing list of facsimile editions and reprints of older titles, see Abebooks (*www.abebooks.com*) and, for free shipping worldwide, The Book Depository (*www.thebookdepository.co.uk*).

Historical context

David Bebbington *Evangelicalism in Modern Britain: A History from the 1730s to the 1980s*. London; Boston: Unwin Hyman, 1989. A fine perspective on Simeon's legacy in its wider context.

Recent works

Derek Prime *Charles Simeon: An ordinary pastor with extraordinary influence* (Day One, 2011). Includes Simeon's sermon on 1 Corinthians 2:2, which forms the basis of his memorial plaque.[41]

Hugh Evan Hopkins *Charles Simeon of Cambridge* (Hodder, 1977). Fully indexed. Now published by Wipf & Stock (USA).

Gary Jenkins *A Tale of Two Preachers: Preaching in the Simeon Stott tradition* (Ridley Hall, Cambridge: Grove Booklets, 2012).[42]

John Stott *Foreword to Evangelical Preaching: An Anthology of Sermons by Charles Simeon* Ed James Houston (Multnomah Press, 1986). Now in 'Classics of Faith and Devotion'.

Older works

A W Brown *Recollections of the Conversation Parties of the Rev Charles Simeon MA with Introductory Notices* (London: Hamilton Adams & Co, 1863).

William Carus *Memoirs of the Life of the Rev. Charles Simeon With a Selection from His Writings and Correspondence.*[43]

Handley Moule *Charles Simeon: Pastor of a Generation (London: Methuen, 1892/Christian Focus, 2001).*

Charles Smyth 'Simeon and Church Order' in *Simeon and Church Order* (Cambridge University Press, 1940).

Arthur Pollard (Ed) *Let Wisdom Judge* (IVP, 1959).

Shorter pieces

Oliver Barclay: *Charles Simeon and the Evangelical Tradition* (1986 Annual Lecture of The Evangelical Library).

Alan Munden sketch of Simeon's theological priorities in *Heart of Faith: Following Christ in the Church of England,* Andrew Atherstone, ed. (Lutterworth, 2008).

John Piper[44] short biographical sketch in *The Roots of Endurance* (Crossway, 2002; IVP Nottingham, 2003).

Vaughan Roberts[44] *In Serving God's Words: Windows on preaching and ministry* by Paul A Barker, Richard J. Condie and Andrew S. Malone, eds. (IVP Nottingham, 2011).

On the life of Henry Martyn

David Bentley-Taylor *My Love Must Wait* (London: IVP, 1975 with later editions).

B V Henry *Forsaking All for Christ: A Biography of Henry Martyn* (London: Chapter Two Trust, 2007).

Constance Padwick *Henry Martyn: Confessor of the Faith* (London: Student Christian Movement, 1922).

John Sargent *Memoir of the Rev. Henry Martyn B.D.* (London: Hatchard 1816 with multiple later editions).

George Smith *Henry Martyn: Saint and Scholar* (London: The Religious Tract Society, 1892).

Related titles by Julia Cameron

Oxford and Cambridge Reformation Walking Tour (Dictum 2018)

John Stott's Right Hand: The untold story of Frances Whitehead (Piquant 2014; Wipf and Stock 2018). A story John Stott himself hoped would one day be told.

John Stott: The humble leader (Christian Focus 2012). To introduce children to 'Uncle John'.

◆ ◆ ◆

ENDNOTES

1. Member of CICCU (Cambridge Inter-Collegiate Christian Union) 1968-71 (Jesus College). The life of the CICCU, threaded through these endnotes, is one part of the longer-term fruit of Simeon's legacy. See Note 21.

2. CICCU College Representative for King's College 1979-80.

3. CICCU President 1986-87 (Selwyn College). Co-founder of '9:38', a UK initiative to train new workers for the harvest fields of Matthew 9:38, 'the other Lord's prayer'. The 'Proc Trust' was founded in 1986 by R C (Dick) Lucas, Rector of St Helen's, Bishopsgate, to strengthen expository preaching. Dick Lucas (Member of CICCU 1947-51; Trinity College, Ridley Hall) was converted through E J H Nash. See Note 21.

4. Never a member of the CICCU, in deference to his father's wishes that he not join, but very active in the movement, and a frequent speaker in college Christian Unions while still a student (Trinity College and Ridley Hall, 1940-1945). CICCU Lifetime Honorary Vice-President.

5. See Arthur Bennett's perceptive article, *Charles Simeon: Prince of Evangelicals* (*Churchman* 102/2 1988), from which the title to this Preface was borrowed.

6. Simeon's memorial stone in the floor of King's Chapel is marked simply 'C.S. 1836'

7. Other positions followed, including Dean of Arts.

8. Advowsons, more commonly referred to now as patronages, could be purchased and sold, as property, until 1898.

9. Homiletics is the study of public preaching, and how to craft and deliver a sermon. The *Horae Homileticae* is a collection of 2,536 sermon outlines, in 21 volumes (Holdsworth and Ball, London). Available now in a facsimile edition from Logos Books.

10. Handley Moule, Simeon's biographer, and later Bishop of Durham, was the first Principal of Ridley Hall. The Hall owns a significant special collection of Simeon archives and effects, and material relating to Henry Martyn; some of this is on permanent loan to Holy Trinity Church and the Henry Martyn Centre. In 2007, Ridley's Simeon Centre was opened with Jane Keiller as Chaplain. Jane served on the staff of Holy Trinity Church from 1980-86, working closely with the CICCU.

11. The story of the 'Cambridge Seven' sent shock-waves through the university community, when six of its most able students, including the England cricketer C T Studd, together with a friend of theirs, joined the China Inland Mission (now known as OMF International), founded in 1865 by Hudson Taylor. This event played a significant role in the surge of mission awareness which was building among students in the CICCU (founded 1877). See also Note 24.

12. The joint Simeon's and Hyndman's Trustees currently oversee the ministries of both Trusts, while they each remain legally separate.

13. Papers available on the Wycliffe Hall website.

14. See William Carus' work in 'Further Reading'. A comprehensive collection for publication is currently in preparation.

15. See Note 23.

16. Another, for example, was Claudius Buchanan, of Queens' College (1766-1815) who campaigned against the Hindu practice of widow burning (suttee). For a concise handling of Buchanan's commitment to Jewish evangelism and the context in which he served, see John S Ross, 'Claudius Buchanan: Scotland's First Missionary to the Jews'

in *Scottish Bulletin of Evangelical Theology*, Edinburgh, May, 2007, vol. 25.1, pp.80-90. See also Note 29.

17. In 1796 Simeon published his first one hundred sermon outlines or 'skeletons', bound with Jean Claude's *Essay on the Composition of a Sermon*. By 1801, five hundred further skeletons were in print.

18. See Appendix 4 for the charge given to new Simeon's Trustees, as they are appointed.

19. College servants who attended to a range of more menial tasks, for students and Fellows. These staff were often long-serving. Simeon's rooms in King's College were above the arch in the Gibbs Building.

20. The Church Mission Society encountered a period of liberal dominance in the early part of the 20th century. In response to this, in 1922, what is now known as Crosslinks was founded.

Handley Moule described Simeon's commitment to Jewish missions as 'perhaps the warmest interest of his life' and 'Literally to the last the thought of the recovery of Israel to the divine Messiah was on Simeon's heart.' (H C G Moule, *Charles Simeon* 1892, reprint. London: IVF, 1948, pp. 95, 96). It was simply 'the most important object in the world' (W T Gidney, *The History of the London Society for Promoting Christianity Amongst the Jews: 1809 - 1908*, London: London Society for Promoting Christianity Amongst the Jews, 1908, p273). Simeon acted on this conviction by helping to found and advocate the work of The London Society for Promoting Christianity among the Jews, now The Church's Ministry among Jewish People (CMJ). His sense of the strategic importance of Jewish evangelism for world mission is well illustrated by a famous incident. After hearing Simeon speak on the subject at a meeting of the London Society, Edward Bickersteth, the secretary of the Church Missionary Society, passed to Simeon a note asking, 'eight millions of Jews and eight hundred million heathens — which is more important?' Simeon's succinct retort, written on the other side of the note, read, 'If the conversion of the eight is life from the dead to the eight hundred, what then?' (Gidney, op cit p273). Bickersteth subsequently became an enthusiastic supporter of Jewish missions, addressing, in all, eighteen anniversary meetings of the London Society. Simeon voiced the hope that the London Society be interdenominational. This did not work out, but it reflects his strategic thinking which proved to be half a century ahead of its time.

21. Simeon's portrait hangs in Blue Boar House, Oxford, the office of the Universities and Colleges Christian Fellowship (UCCF). UCCF's founding movement, the CICCU, could never have been imagined in Simeon's lifetime, yet Simeon's influence can be clearly traced as a tributary to its founding.

It was required in Simeon's day that all Cambridge University students agree to the 39 Articles of the Church of England, which then excluded all non-conformists. While students were obliged to attend college chapel, there was no spiritual vitality to be found in their cloisters. To attend worship at Holy Trinity Church, and be known as a 'Sim' or 'Simeonite' was, in the words of Oliver Barclay (Trinity College 1938-45; a wartime CICCU President, second General Secretary of the Inter-Varsity Fellowship [now UCCF]) 'a passport to contempt'. Barclay sums up the contributing factors to the founding of the CICCU as:

(i) Simeon's influence on many ordinands, called to parishes around the country, which led to more and more evangelical families choosing to send their sons to Cambridge. Through worshipping at Holy Trinity these younger generation students got to know one another;

(ii) The Jesus Lane Sunday School, which led in turn to the founding of three significant prayer movements: (a) the Cambridge Union for Private Prayer (1848), to pray for those training for ministry; (b) the Cambridge University Church Missionary Union (1858), to pray for missionaries, and students considering serving overseas; (c) the Daily Prayer Meeting (DPM) formed in 1862 by two freshers [US: freshmen], who had prayed daily at school. Their school meeting had been encouraged by their headmaster – a former teacher at the Jesus Lane Sunday School.

In 1871, all religious tests were removed from university entrance, and nonconformists began to come to Cambridge. The founding of the CICCU in 1877 led to an evangelical witness to Christ being established in each of the Cambridge colleges. This in turn led, in God's grace, to the planting of Christian Unions in universities across the UK. Through the work of the International Fellowship of Evangelical Students (IFES, founded 1947) the story continues to unfold with sister movements of UCCF now in over 155 nations. An excellent treatment of this is found in *From Cambridge to the World* by Oliver R Barclay and Robert M Horn (IVP Nottingham, 2002).

In his early eighties, John Stott reflected on contemporary movements which had shaped him spiritually. There were two, he said: 'Iwerne and the CICCU'. As a newly-converted schoolboy, he was drawn into leadership of Iwerne camps, founded by E J H Nash, better known as 'Bash'. (The camps, for British public schoolboys, took their name from Iwerne Minster where they were originally held. They are now known as 'Iwerne Holidays', organized by the Titus Trust.) Nash was himself a Cambridge graduate (Trinity College and Ridley Hall, 1922-27) and a CICCU man, again bringing us back to the influence of Simeon.

22. Simeon was an Old Etonian; Stott a Rugbeian. Both placed high value on ministry among students, occupying pulpits in major university towns. John Stott's dates as follows: Rugby School (1935-1940); Trinity College, Cambridge (1940-1942); Ridley Hall, Cambridge (1942-1945); All Souls Church, Langham Place, London (Curate 1945-1950; Rector 1950-1975; Rector Emeritus 1975-2011).

'Uncle John', as Stott was affectionately known by thousands of younger friends around the world, spoke of Simeon's influence on his ministry, and asked for the same concise, declaratory wording on the memorial plaque at Holy Trinity Church (see inside back cover) to be engraved in due course on his own memorial stone. This now stands, in Welsh slate, in the churchyard of St James the Great, Dale, Pembrokeshire, near his writing retreat, The Hookses.

23. The clear commitment of men like Wilberforce and Shaftesbury to the alleviation of poverty gradually became lost among western evangelicals. As theological liberalism took root, evangelicals focused on preserving a high view of scripture in the Church; and as decades passed, social concern became regarded as 'a social gospel' more identified with liberal theology. The realignment of doctrinal orthodoxy with 'orthopraxy' is widely attributed to the influence of two Latin American theologians, Samuel Escobar (b. Peru 1934) and René Padilla (b. Ecuador 1932) at the 1974 International Congress on World Evangelization, held in Lausanne, Switzerland, convened by the American evangelist, Billy Graham. From this gathering issued *The Lausanne Covenant*, a groundbreaking document; and today's Lausanne Movement.

24. John Stott's successor – in fashioning The Lausanne Movement's major *Cape Town Commitment* (issuing from The Third Lausanne Congress, Cape Town 2010) – was Christopher J H Wright, International Director, Langham Partnership. Chris Wright served as Executive Secretary for the CICCU (1967-68) and as CICCU Coll Rep for St Catharine's College in the previous year.

On his death in 2011, John Stott was succeeded as Lausanne Movement Honorary Chair by Michael Cassidy, founder of African Enterprise. Michael was converted to Christ in his first term at St Catharine's College and a member of the CICCU 1955-58. He acknowledges the lasting impact on him, as a student, of the final sentence of John Pollock's classic book *The Cambridge Seven*, namely: 'This is a story of ordinary men, and may thus be repeated.' John Pollock (1924-2012), viewed by many as perhaps the finest Christian biographer of his generation was also a CICCU man.

25. Parallels have also been drawn with William Still (1911-1997), Minister of Gilcomston South Church of Scotland, Aberdeen, for 52 years (1945-1997), and noted for (i) the passion of his preaching, which at first brought opposition; (ii) his investing in students; (iii) his mark on the growth of expository preaching in Scotland; and (iv) his desire in his lifetime to effect change from within the established Church. Like Charles Simeon, Willie Still began his ministry with no obvious human teacher.

26. See specific references in *A Tale of Two Preachers: Preaching in the Simeon-Stott Tradition* by Gary Jenkins: Chapter 2. For a more comprehensive treatment, see the seminal two-volume authorized biography of John Stott: *John Stott: The Making of a Leader* and *John Stott: A Global Ministry* by his friend and contemporary Timothy Dudley-Smith. (Nottingham, England and Downers Grove, IL: IVP, 1999, 2000.)

27. LICC has been led since 1999 by Mark Greene (Trinity Hall 1974-78) whose conversion to Christ from his Jewish roots may be traced, under God, to friends at university.

28. Henry Martyn left a mark on world mission to which no justice can be done in an endnote. This portrait now hangs in the Holy Trinity Church Office, with a copy above the fireplace in the Henry Martyn Hall, built in 1887, adjoining the church. Another copy hangs in St John's College. Martyn was Senior Wrangler (top mathematician of his year) and received the university Latin prize. Yet he left behind not only the prestige of an academic career, but also his beloved fiancée, Lydia Grenfell, whom he could not persuade to accompany him, to sail for India. His health failed not long after he arrived, and he died aged 31 in Tokat, Armenia, now Northern Turkey. But in those brief, difficult, seven years, he translated the whole of the New Testament into Urdu, Persian, Judaeo-Persian and Arabic. He also translated the Psalms into Persian and the *Book of Common Prayer* into Urdu. A plaque to his memory may be found on the south wall of the chancel in Holy Trinity. See Hugh Evan Hopkins. *Op cit* p149.

A Trust was established in Henry Martyn's name in 1881, initially to raise funds for constructing the Henry Martyn Hall. A missionary library for university students was proposed, in his memory, to 'help build up a true sense of the importance of Missions in those who will afterwards hold the highest offices both in Church and State'. The library opened in 1898. In 1982, Michael Rees, then vicar of Holy Trinity, appointed John Cooper as the first Henry Martyn Advisor, to work with students who were exploring the possibility of overseas service. Canon Graham Kings, later to become Bishop of Sherborne, was appointed in 1992 as Henry Martyn Lecturer in Missiology in the Cambridge Theological Federation, and under his leadership, the library moved to Westminster College, as part of the Cambridge University Theological Federation. This coincided with a rapid growth in academic study of world Christianity. In its centenary year, 1998, the Henry Martyn Library took the new name Henry Martyn Centre, to reflect its broader ministry. Today the Centre continues to promote openings for graduates in academic research, or to serve overseas, either under the aegis of evangelical mission agencies, or in a professional capacity. Thus it fulfils the aim of its original founders in 1898.

For a fine summary of Henry Martyn's contribution to world mission, and to its academic study, see Graham Kings's 2012 lecture for the Cambridge Theological Federation and Henry Martyn Centre: 'Missionary Scholar for our Age' (29 February

2012). Graham Kings introduces Martyn's two converts; other missionaries of particular influence in India at the time; and several later missionaries inspired by Henry Martyn's story. He further traces reflections of Martyn's life in the writing of Samuel Taylor Coleridge, George Eliot, Charlotte Brontë, and relates how it surfaced in a childhood reminiscence of Jeanette Winterson. A free download with audio option is available on the Henry Martyn Centre website.

Patrick Brontë (Charlotte's father) - a student at St John's where Henry Martyn was a Fellow - had been influenced in his choice of Haworth by Simeon. In that parish from 1742-1763 William Grimshaw, a friend of John Wesley, had left a significant mark on which he could build. (Some editions of Charlotte Brontë's *Jane Eyre* note the character of St John Rivers as based on Henry Martyn.)

29. Martyn was also, by this stage, vicar of Lolworth Parish Church, five miles northwest of Cambridge. Charles Simeon maintained a profound long-term commitment to missions in India. Prior to the appointment of Anglican Bishops and the legalization of missionary work in the East India Company Charter of 1813, Simeon actively recruited, usually in consultation with Charles Grant, the six chaplains known collectively as the Evangelical Chaplains: David Brown, Claudius Buchanan, Henry Martyn, Daniel Corrie, Joseph Parson, and Thomas Thomason. Martyn and Thomason in particular worked closely with Simeon prior to their departure, with Thomason assisting Simeon extensively during a several-year period when poor health did not permit Simeon to fulfil preaching commitments. Simeon later provided valuable assistance in looking after family matters in Britain to which the Chaplains could not attend. After the establishment of Anglican dioceses in India, Simeon continued to recruit missionaries and chaplains. Late in his life, reflecting on his recruitment and unofficial oversight of so many ministers, he mused, 'It merely shows how early God enabled me to act for India, to provide for which has now for forty-one years been a principal and an incessant object of my care and labour .... I used jocosely to call India my *Diocese*. Since there has been a Bishop, I modestly call it my *Province*.' See H C G Moule, *Charles Simeon* (London: Methuen, 1892, p111.)

30. A Ministry of Word and Prayer: What can we learn from Charles Simeon today? In *Serving God's Words: Windows on preaching and ministry* edited by Paul A Barker, Richard J Condie and Andrew S Malone. Nottingham, England: IVP, 2011. (Published as a *Festschrift* for Peter Adam.)

31. *The Oxford Pastorate* by G Ian F Thomson (London: The Canterbury Press, 1946) p35.

32. *Charles Simeon of Cambridge* by Hugh Evan Hopkins (London: Hodder and Stoughton, 1977) p86.

In rejoicing in his church-based ministry, Simeon's loyalty lay squarely with the Church of England, and effecting change from within. (See Hopkins p213; Moule p166.) Contemporary movements now mirroring this would be Reform (UK) and Anglican Mainstream (Anglican Communion).

33. Simeon had commissioned the portrait, painted in Calcutta, which had been delivered to India House. 'It was completed after Martyn had finished his Hindustani translation of the New Testament and before he set out on his final journey from India, through Persia, to perfect his Persian and Arabic translations of the New Testament.' (See Graham Kings's lecture 'Missionary Scholar for our Age'.)

34. Calvinism is based on the teaching of the French theologian John Calvin (1509-1564); Arminianism on the teaching of the Dutch theologian Jacobus Arminius (1560-1609) . In brief, salvation rests for the Arminian on the basis of the individual's free choosing; for the Calvinist on the basis of God's election.

35. As Simeon described himself in the Preface to his *Horae Homileticae*.

36. One was St Edward's; the other the Church of the Holy Sepulchre, known as the Round Church, where Christian Heritage is now based. The vicar at the time of Simeon's conversation was Henry William Coulthurst (incumbent 1782-90).

    More recently: following the remarkable ministry of Mark Ruston from 1955, in which the church grew significantly, Mark Ashton (vicar from 1987; died 2010) moved the congregation to the then redundant building of St Andrew the Great (StAG). This church, from 2011 under the leadership of Alasdair Paine, continues to flourish. All three vicars were active in the CICCU as undergraduates. (See *Persistently Preaching Christ*. Ed: Christopher Ash, Mary Davis and Bob White. CFP: 2012.)

37. Simeon recorded this conversation in the third person, in his *Expository Outlines on the Whole Bible*, Vol. 1: Genesis-Leviticus Preface, pp xvii-xviii. Wesley's journal entry is found in *The Journal of the Rev John Wesley, A.M. Enlarged from original MSS, with notes from unpublished diaries, annotations, maps, and illustrations.* Ed. Nehemiah Curock, (London: The Epworth Press, 1938), vol. viii, p39f.

38. He was known in the US as August Edouart. *Catalogue of 3,800 named and dated American silhouette portraits by August Edouart* (edited and published by Emily Jackson, b. 1861, the year Edouart died) is available through online retailers.

39. Timothy Dudley-Smith, John Stott's authorized biographer; hymnwriter; Bishop of Thetford (1981-91), served as CICCU Treasurer 1946-47 and Vice-President 1947-48.

40. The material for Appendices 1-3 by kind permission of Ridley Hall (see Acknowledgments).

41. Derek Prime (Emmanuel College) served as Secretary to John Stott's first Cambridge mission (1952), and then as CICCU Secretary (1952-53).

42. Gary Jenkins's lucid and rich-in-substance 28pp booklet from the Grove Spirituality Series forms an excellent sequel to this short work. It looks first at the shared endeavours of these two Cambridge Anglicans, then examines their preaching methods, and evaluates these methods for contemporary culture.

43. Simeon's curate, who succeeded him as vicar in 1836.

44. John Piper and Vaughan Roberts were expositors at The Third Lausanne Congress on World Evangelization, with Ramez Atallah (Egypt), Ruth Padilla Deborst (El Salvador), Ajith Fernando (Sri Lanka) and Calisto Odede (Kenya). John Stott, unable to travel, sent a written greeting to the Congress, as did Billy Graham.

45. Artist unknown. Taken from George Smith: *Henry Martyn: Saint and Scholar* (1892). The quotation is one of six 'sayings' to appear on the reverse of the 1906 memorial card (pp36-37). The 'last remaining chorister', T H Case, did not include his name, stating only 'St Leonards-on-Sea'.

HOLY TRINITY CHURCH IN 1803

'The sun and moon are scarcely more separated from each other than Cambridge is from what it was when I was first Minister at Trinity Church.' (Charles Simeon, 1823)[45]

CONTRIBUTORS

John E Benton: Gained a science PhD before being called into the ministry. He pastored a church in Guildford, Surrey from 1980 for 36 years and is now Director of Pastoral Support for the Pastors' Academy at London Seminary. John is married to Ann. He is editor of the monthly newspaper *Evangelicals Now*.

Julia E M Cameron: Member of Holy Trinity Church, Cambridge in the early 1980s. Served from 1981 with UCCF, OMF International, IFES and the Lausanne Movement. Now Director of Publishing for the Lausanne Movement, and a member of St Ebbe's Church, Oxford.

Canon R Michael Rees (1935-2018): Trustee of Simeon's Trust (1969-1999), Vicar of Holy Trinity Church, Cambridge (1972-1984), Chief Secretary of Church Army (1984-1990), Moderator, Evangelism Committee of the British Council of Churches (1985-1988), Canon Missioner in Chester Diocese (1990-2000).

Acknowledgments

Our special thanks to Elaine Thornton for giving access to Ridley Hall's collection of Simeon archives, and Henry Martyn archival material; and to Peter Monteith (King's College), Kathryn McKee (St John's College) and Krista Siemens (Cambridge University Library) for their kind help.

Our thanks, too, to Gordon Ogilvie, David Bailey and Ann Brown (*Simeon's Trustees*); Rupert Charkham, Abby Ringer and Bethany Cragg (*Holy Trinity Church, Cambridge*); Timothy Dudley-Smith (*retired Bishop of Thetford*); Emma Wild-Wood, Lucy Hughes and Jane Gregory (*Henry Martyn Centre*); Andrew Atherstone and Simon Vibert (*Wycliffe Hall, Oxford*); Paula Elliott (*St Peter's Free Church, Dundee*); Jill Spink (*Cascadas, Spain*); Liz Leahy (*Azusa Pacific University, California*); Joe Martin (*St Ebbe's Church, Oxford*); Scott Ayler (*University of Sharjah, UAE*); John Ross (*retired Free Church minister, Drumnadrochit*); Andrew Roberts (*Trumpington Local History Group*).

Further, we wish to honour the biographers of Charles Simeon and Henry Martyn, whose works have been cited.